These Humans

Steven Schild

Up On Big Rock Poetry Series
SHIPWRECKT BOOKS PUBLISHING COMPANY

IN®
DIE

Cover photos by Steven Schild
Cover & interior design by Shipwreckt Books

Contents

Epitaph

Between black lines,
tell my children
how I smiled
in the gleeful June sun,
lounged naked and human
in my woman's candle eyes.
Tell them of a blue river
and a white boat,
a short swim
one stunning afternoon
when I nearly drowned
but didn't.

I. The Days

Lament for Grant Smith, Kahler Hotel Porter, Long Deceased

Terrible teeth.
Too little care,
too many cigarettes,
too much strong drink
poured over what once was white
and then ceased to be,
as did he
who I knew briefly
through graveyard shifts in
grimy white smocks,
garish grey slacks,
bland black shoes,
one size fitting all,
seldom too small but even if not
never right.

I bet if we went back
to that locker room where the chef,
wearing only his crestfallen cap,
warned me not to eat those day-old rolls
if they'd sat even for a second
on the sway-backed bench that had borne
so many tired behinds all those years,
I bet we'd still sense, maybe even see,
the signature smoke rings he blew
through the O of that mouth
that held those terrible teeth
that once had to be
white as his youth.

Tillman Park in January

No light but that left
by the dotage of dusk;

no sound save the cutting song
of skate blade, the plunk of puck
on plywood boards;

no cold good gloves
can't keep out, no wind
longjohns won't ward off:

This playground rink is a
planet unto itself,
perfect,
and the lone stickman here
glides in a singular orbit
with nothing between him
and the nirvana of empty net,
a soul skating circles in heaven.

These Humans
for G & J C

From her wheelchair
she clowned with the kids
trailing behind her husband,
who shoved the grocery cart
through crowded aisles
while her legs, the legs that
brought those children here,
lie dead in front of her;
she smiled all the while.

With his wife dying
he wrote about peaches and cream,
resurrecting from childhood
sugary truths about gardens
and all they bring us,
crates of cling peaches
fuzzy and packed in crinkly pink paper,
and between the lines was the lip-smacking smile
of a man who loved home-grown tomatoes,
cucumbers, radishes, cabbage, raspberries
and knew how to bring them forth
from the earth that he knew
would soon cover his bride.

Nearby,
we three laughed as one recited
by heart, "Death plucked me by the ear;
'Listen,' he said—'I'm coming,'"
each of us threescore gone
or nearly so, we who had just remarked

about the gorgeous autumn day;
knowing what was coming,
we laughed anyway.

What creatures they be!
What creatures are we,
these humans, holding tight
to the sweetness of yesterday,
knowing what is coming
we laugh anyway,
each on his own, walking away,
glimmers on an autumn day,
laughing like children
'till tomorrow has its say.

Something for a Son

A man awash in womanness
awaiting the outcome
of an act of love,
lone man attending the birth.
My heart is in the right place
but my equipment is all wrong,
all thumbs, all arms and elbows
in this hothouse of skyward-knifing knees
and heart-shaped hips, this garden
of women in which I can do nothing
for my son but say this:

"Be stronger of heart
than of arm.
Be first to extend a hand
after anger.
Neither run from thunder
nor take lightning lightly.
Look life in the eye.
Behold and believe
all that is good.
Be ready for the rest.
Be worth all this.
Be worth all this."

Little League

"He hits like the dickens—really spanks the ball. And he's only 11." —Doting father

Soon will come
the curve,
seductive sleight of hand
that puts a knife's edge
on the round ball and makes it fall
straight away,

and then, worse yet,
the flashing lie that is
the slider, darting snake
that sends big hackers back home
broken, with no notion of
what hit them.

So, little one,
love the game,
you gleaming boy
of brown brow
and glistening skin
and green grass stains
that never come out,

so love the game
while the ball flies straight
and very close to true,
the one bound to burn by
in the bat of an eye.

Russell Square Park (London, 6-29-11)

The young gorge themselves
on hot dogs and cigarettes
and each other;
the not-young trundle through,
running from what can't be escaped
or sitting to summon or save
the strength to face it.

Weighed down by what we know,
we fill up like sacks and
seep out like balloons
in slow leaks or whooshes,
we surrender to our appetites and illusions;
together here we sing our singular tunes
fulfilling our fates perfectly,
getting and spending,
coming and going,
blind, blithe, foolish, knowing,
chasing what can't be caught,
learning what can't be taught.

It is, as the scorpion would say,
without sense, but it is our way,
it is how we have our tiny say,
the daunting beauty
of the cloud-dappled day.

On Cretin Avenue

More striking still
than her sun-suckled thighs
was the fear
in the dark-haired
young woman's eyes,
was the cast of her gaze
quickly down and away
as she walked toward
a stranger
that gorgeous
fall day.

I hurt
for her father,
I sigh
for my son
for the love
to be lost
in all those
like this one
who stares at
soiled sidewalk,
regards rubbish,
rough stone,
for fear
of looking up
and being worse than alone.

Lessons

Philip Senn taught me
while coaching a team
that never won anything
that the catcher should always
make a good throw back to
the pitcher so the pitcher
can save his juice
for pitching.

My dad taught me
when we were hale and hearty
never to complain about getting old
because the only way to avoid it
is dying young.

My mom taught me
as we folded laundry
that even the tiniest kindness,
even something so small that
most would never notice,
is worth "Thank you,"
which costs nothing at all.

The leaves on the ground teach me
that fall has begun but is not over, and that it
is beautiful though we know what
follows may not be,
and that the specks
of sunshine that come even
with the last of it are
parts of the story, too,

perhaps the parts most true,
whatever that is, and,
ordinary though they be,
perhaps most important of all
for all to say, for all to see.

Imprint: High Ways and Low

Slope of the shoulders,
width of the back,
weight of the forearms,
girth of the neck:
I am defined in the dust of ancient tracks.
It is in the sinew, in the loins:
I am my father's arms
and his hands.

Scowl of the visage,
straining of wrist,
jut of the jawbone,
tension of fist:
I am weighted in the mire of ancient ruts.
It is in the marrow, in the cells:
I am my father's elbows
and his knees.

How Quickly It Goes

How quickly it goes,
how soon the first seeds
of moustache bud above
the still-girlish beauty's
unknowing lips,
how soon the shortstop,
still a boy,
cheats a step closer to home
because of what's already gone
from his arm,
how soon even the young
and those who lament
no longer being so,
how soon they,
how soon we all
kiss so much goodbye.

After Tending Flowers at My Parents' Grave

In sunlight we raced uphill
away from the headstones
toward the waiting car,
his lead lengthening one long, strong stride
after another, and me unable to make up
any ground, watching his shoe bottoms
churn up and down
and his blonde hair shine, first son
of mine speeding ahead to stay.

And though startled to lose
quite that soon, quite that way,
the old man to himself had to smile and say
he sure did look handsome
pulling away.

Front Pages the Day after Prince Died

Just for the time it takes to flip a page,
let's wipe Flint's poisoned water away,
let's let Syria's rivers of blood run
elsewhere so we can sing and cry about
he who played guitar perhaps like no other,
he who fiddled while the world burned,
fiddled so we could for a verse or two
forget Flint's poisoned water and Syria's blood

and marvel at who was this Prince—this hero
or star or tail of a comet blazing by and taking us with him
away from the world and into deep space
where sound waves live forever
in any ear willing and wanting to hear.

Child Fear

This is as real as any god,
this trembling
that comes with
washing hair
and the horror
of soap in the eyes,
panic brought on by pets
and department-store
Santa Clauses, clowns
in small-town parades.
No "There, there," no warm kiss
can make it not be so,
not this, as real as any god,
crying itself out
in a world where
cars squash squirrels
on sunny days
while wee ones
go about their play
with cars the size
of candy bars
and psyches made of clay
and wait and wish
and hope to have
this horror
go away.

Grandpa's Potatoes

"When you put that little bugger in the ground,"
Grandpa taught us,
"point the eye at the sky,"
let the seed face the sun.
 "Why make it work harder
than it has to? Give it a head start
and chances are better
it'll feed you."

And if it does,
"Eat the skin, too—
it's the best part for you"
no matter how rough or dirty
that brown coat once was—he knew
how comfortable work-worn clothes can be,
denim and flannel that looked like they'd never been new,
clothes that fit him like skin as he sat at the supper table,
dirt still under his fingernails,
eating fat potatoes and doubtless smiling
to himself at the way he knew the world
and that potato's eye
and the way it all tasted
from the ground to the sky.

And There You Are

One fine day
all that stuff
all those old people
have always told young people
comes true,

and there you are,
the flower of your youth
on the floor around you
like desiccated petals,

and there you are,
a stem,
a stalk,
 a stub
of what you once were,

another old fart
possessed by a truth
that has to be told and,
as long as it can be,
ignored.

What I Remember Most about Phoenix

What I remember most about Phoenix
is the bandanna'd crazyman
screaming nonstop on his corner
except for ten minutes on the hour
to drink bottled water in the shade
while tourists and conventioneers ignored him
and he, screaming all he was good for,
ignored their ignoring him, all going
about their business as if nobody else were there

and as if the desert were not so near, as if
the Gila monsters and the rest of the reptiles
did not know, through their sand-burnished bellies,
that the commotion these strangers were causing
wouldn't last long, as if the lizards big and small
didn't go about their business
cold-blooded as sunshine on sand.

We Do What We Can

We do what we can:
comb over bald spots,
slither into shapewear,
don dark clothes to hide
those parts we wish
were not there,
those parts we would
love to lose or have lost. And still,

we are what we are, each
a singularly human star
or light lesser by far but light no less,
one among many, all

somehow on fire and by that fire
consumed, each a singularly human star
in and of itself and by itself bound,
each a singularly human star
from which the one at the center
never ventures too far.

And the rest—the regret and the rest
we idle past every day like the wallpaper of our lives,
noticing only every now and then, and,
upon noticing, taking stock and moving on,
shrugging and vaguely knowing

that we are what we are,
each a singularly human star.

II. The Natural World

Fountain City Sunset

Sunshine on brown brick;
sunshine on green paint;
sunshine on lathe-turned wood:
The river is high,
a sated snake with
muddy brown skin,
banks a-bulge with
all it holds in;
the leaves are on fire
with the sigh of summer past;
towering stone faces
a crimson smile cast
on trains below,
like toys chugging past.

Runner

The sweat had barely dried
from the swelter of July
when crisp leaves crackled
underfoot as the runner pounded
up hill and over flat
with only the smallest step off track
here and there to dodge a stray nail,
duck a threatening branch, run around
a road kill. One
step at a time, one
foot always about to fall, one
leg straining ahead of the other, lungs
dry as leaves, autumn
sure as shoes wear out when
soles pound the ground again
and again in this thinning air, this
gravity where
even the strongest falls behind
in trying to stay in step
with time.

Oratorio

for Dick & Karen Hastings

The requiem ended; the preacher went home.
The singers disrobed and took down risers,
and the church echoed with the commotion of
friends killing time till it was time to go.
Kids ran squealing from crying room
to altar and back again,
women chatted about children teaching
on one coast or having babies
on another, men marveled in
unmusical tones about the beauty
of the notes that had flown
through the stained-glass glow
to the vaulted arches and
washed back down again as warmth
that landed and lounged in the vacant pews
where rested God in His everyday clothes.

Beatitude: Cycle of Water

for Corrine Arneson Schild

These are the women who rise
before the sun in winter
to coax warmth
from cast-iron woodstoves
left untended all night.

These are the women who stand
over cauldrons of coffee,
the spattering fury of bacon,
the mad sizzle of red meat.

These are the women who reach
raw hands into roaring ovens,
rescue cakes, loaves of bread.

These are the women who hover
like dreams over feverish children,
bringers of blanket, bringers of broth,
wielders of water, soothing damp cloth:

These are the women,
the women unseen,
invisible as vapor,
powerful as steam,
the women of men
once young
and consumed with fire.

Nightly News

for John Berryman, Henry, the eminent Dr. Bones

"A satellite circled striated Jupiter
from a quarter-million miles away
and sent back photos
technicians will splice together
to study the planet's composition.
It is speculated that Earth's atmosphere
was similar in its early stages,
but we know virtually nothing
about this largest planet,
only that it has thirteen moons
and, just south of its equator, a mysterious
red blotch three times the circumference of Earth.

"Closer to home,
a Portage farmer, a 'quiet family man
with no financial problems and an
outstanding work record,'
shotgunned his wife and sons
last night, then turned the gun on himself.
He had been despondent lately, 'sick to death
of winter. All we can figure out,' intoned the coroner,
'is that the weather was getting him down.'

"Also yesterday, authorities made official
the death of young Chester Metcalfe, who
'clung precariously to life,' battled irreversible
brain damage more than two days after being discovered

frozen in a snowbank. There was no visible
evidence of a struggle or injury."

All of these investigators and scientists puzzled
while the four of us sprawl here drunk
even before the bourbon, half-buzzed
by the nightly news but seeing clearly as any

that on this inauspicious day it rained,
first rain of Spring (so it is called, but
Someone may be teasing; we weren't
convinced because the rain kept on freezing).

Should we tell them, boys, should we give them
a measure on the world and the weather?
—No; it's like the price of a yacht,
a luxury, this knowing—if you gotta ask . . .

Let's have another drink;
let's sigh and be certain
there is only this season,
have a laugh while they try
to coax us sober with Reason.

On an Upstairs Window

It looked like sculpture,
swirls of ice etched on glass by
Jack Frost's pretty knife.

From One Who Eats Meat

Put a good knife to a fresh kill and marvel,
through the escaping steam, at the way it perfectly lays back
hide and muscle and cuts straight to the heart of the matter,
the viscera, that which minutes ago was alive and on the hoof and
aloof to or unlucky with what might have been a clean, perfect shot,
an epiphany of powder and slug in a wood that had been quiet
but for the stalking, the struggles, the kills we are not part of.

Ask the butchered elk if he feels at one with the one who
killed him, the one who shot him true and dead; ask the woods
that have no ears for the pretty tales we tell whether
there is any compact here, any bargain, any evening,
or whether this chain of being is nothing but
surrender to the hungry belly's growl
that rumbles in us all.

Great Dakota Gathering and Homecoming

Right off the bike path
running through the heart of the park
a piece of polished stone promises
"Otakuye hdihunipi,"
truth and atonement, it says,
in a language we do not know.

"Reconsiliation" (spelled wrong)
and "Dakota Bingo"
under the same roof,
a synthetic white tent
tied down with metal stakes,
held up by a skeleton
of aluminum poles.

Smoke rising from the drum ritual
is from cigarettes long, white, menthol;
the game is sticks whacking skins
on a plywood base, the drummers
brown-skinned, pony-tailed, tattooed.

To steal from the Kiowa who wrote about
the Hopi view of the white man's rules and schools,
there is no center to it;
  "All relatives have come," the stone promises,
but it is buried neck-deep so we cannot see
what lies beneath—rusted remnants
of musket ball and broken bones,
clubs that smashed spines and skulls,
arrows that blinded eyes;

we can know no more of what came before
than we can lead ghosts to gallows—
the past is a house that was
and can no longer be;
we cannot rebuild it
or live in it overnight
or find our way to or from.

This is as close as we get:
Celebration, proclamation,
white men in feathers
stumbling to stay in step with the drum,
Indians proud, fierce and foolish
in the uniform that killed them,
wine in paper cups,
curlicues carved in stone,
statuary bidding us remember
what we can never know
as we amble through
barely breaking a sweat.

American Indian Studies, Phoenix

Inside,
papers, podia,
elevated elocutions,
pontification on
sacred and profane;
pinstripes, neckties, khakis,
ponytails, bald spots,
spectacles,
stares
into space.

Outside,
desert, vacant places
seen and unseen,
reptile smile
caring little how little
it matters
what we latecomers
here presume to do.

Pacific City, Oregon, June 14, 2014

Colors bright
against low-tide grey,
squealing children
high-tail it for the waves,
squishing between toes
of flipper-like feet
sand that is the remnant
of stone ground tiny by time:
the ocean,
the ocean

and what it washes up:
exoskeleton, claw, shells
in smithereens, leavings that survived
from creatures that did not.

It draws us back,
it stops us in our tracks
soon washed away,
it draws us back
amazed in the wreckage of what was
and the beauty of what is,
therein to rejoice and wonder
and then, one day, fine or otherwise, somewhere
near here or another place like this,
to die, the ceaseless sound of the sea
the last thing we know.

Backwaters on Bartlett Lake

for Dave Miller

Bugs walk on water;
fish we won't catch ignore us;
sun-fired lilies yawn.

Shameless dragonflies
mate in midair, their congress
shimmering blue heat.

Stoned on sun, turtles
line logs, waiting for nothing:
Here there is no time.

III. The Women

Breakfast

for Margaret Canney Schild and Corrine Arneson Schild

As if to make more of the ordinary eggs,
to splash color before a sun not quite up,
she sliced peppers, orange, red and yellow,
and, to lend a savor so slight and earthy and elemental
that we crave it without knowing,
she sprinkled musky mushroom morsels,
stirring it all together standing in one spot,
hips dancing though she never took a step.

And then,
having watched it sizzle over the fire
till it was done but still little more than
a frypan of eggs, she garnished it with a
benediction of, "It's ready, boys."
So blessed,
we began our day.

Mother

Rhythm of rocker,
wicker chair,
comforting creak
on hardwood floor,
bygone yawn of
sleeping boy
who need cry
in the night
no more.

For Such Women

Sure as night comes,
she grows every day
rounder, whiter
in this heart,
this house, busy
with potting soil
and seed,
using soft words
and dustcloth
to keep out all
that does not belong here,
imparting to every surface
a shine she calls common.

Women are stronger.
Not with an army of knives
could I keep as safe this house
as does the armor
of her cotton dress.

"Lanesville, 1958"

A poem after a photograph by Saul Leiter

Nothing on but a
shadow camouflaging one breast
and sunlight showing off the other as if
a display-window bauble behind which passes that
part of the world that meets the eye
without looking back, which I cannot
do as you sprawl sun-basted in that wicker chair
wearing
nothing but a shadow, you and your furry bush
lounging queen-like, dream-like on the
mantle made by the curving line of an
empty foreground chair; you are there
forever in that old film, filament, firmament,
naked but for hair primped in curls with
light streaming in and the
world loafing by, you of the sinewy arm
and glistening thigh, wearing nothing
but a shadow camouflaging one breast
and light lapping at the other
sweet fruit from which we draw desire so strong
that it lasts as long as you have lasted lounging
perfectly there in "Lanesville, 1958" with
nothing on but a
shadow camouflaging one breast
and . . .

One Verse of Rachel Robinson's Lament

"He was" —she went silent, searching for the right
word— "expressive." Jackie Robinson's widow Rachel in
a Ken Burns interview

She missed that man's hands on her,
missed those broad shoulders, missed being
wrapped up in those meaty arms
and sturdy legs that never let her go
even when long gone.

What the DJ Sees

It is a dark word:
peligrosa—means danger
y es la verdad—
and it is the truth.

In it women dance—
arms like branches, legs like trees;
they sway, swivel and sweat.

We men watch like dogs—
we want them all, all the time,
all of them and none.

Lights say we must leave—
the steady, low thrum of drums
sets our teeth on edge.

In a Stranger's Bathroom

No place else
on this beautiful planet
will my nose be as close
to your naked nether
as in this musky room
where damp towels
dangle and tile
sweats.

Behind the shadowy
shower curtain
water courses
unabashed down
your luscious form,
finds every nook,
every fold,
every secret
to be told in the
curve of a belly,
in the small of a back.

Letter to a Lover

Say this heart is a lake.
Say you pilot your white canoe
over the dark water,
peering down in as far as you can see.
And say you find your spot, bait
your hook and angle for one worth
taking home--
but before dropping anchor
ask yourself and answer
what you might catch
and what you dare keep,
whether the open-mouthed weirdness
of these queer fish
might set a hook
you can't pull free
and send you back
rowing like hell for solid ground.

We Watch Our Women Bloom

We watch our women bloom:
seed, blossom, flower, our
girlfriends, lovers, wives, mothers

and their deepening cycles,
widening circles, separate slices
of rounding fruit, more today
than yesterday, more tomorrow
than we know, certain as seasons
come and go--monument, mirror,
memento, morsel of the time we
first took up, first touched, first
thought we knew.

We Fall in Love

We fall in love
and take up with
we know not what
or truly who;
we have some sense of
look and feel and heart
but know nothing
of what is to be,
of what is under that young skin
and how it, how we, will hold up
under the years

into which we stride
step in step, side by side
with shoulders hunched
against winter
or bared to bask in
high summer,
on the strong legs of youth
making our way away from
young, toward what
will come, stride for stride,
side by side with this one
not long ago the stranger
we fell for, the one
we hold onto
not knowing where we're going,
not knowing what we lose
if we let go.

IV. The War

He Loved to Play Ball

"They stuck me at first"
on his summer-league softball team
because he couldn't throw like he used to
after the shoulder didn't rehab right,
the shoulder he fucked up when,
doing in animal panic what he was told to do,
he jumped out the back of the truck
and landed wrong, he who two months ago
was bored so bad he could barely sit still
surrounded by all those girls and all that bullshit
at school, he who so loved to play ball,
a moon-faced boy who signed up
and got what he never expected to get
when he lost it
in the field at Fallujah.

At the Embassy Ball

The sultans have their say,
and then in their sultanly way
rejoin the banquet,
elegant pens and pins shining
idly, jewelry catching
the gleaming lights, ties and gowns
beaming like flags. Young men in fine livery
bring, on elegant trays, cocktails, coffee and
sweets; amid the clinking gaiety,
over the susurration of glistening lips is
what sounds like muffled guns
comfortably distant.

Written Upon Reading the Obituary of Vo Nguyen Giap (1911-2013)

You can put a suit on this old knife man,
you can teach him to eat with the right fork
and not spit at the table

but you'll never get out of his hair the itch of long-gone mud,
never get out of his wispy moustache the scent of the shit he slept in,
never get out of his shrunken belly the growl of hunger
that fed him longer than we can remember.
You can butter him up until the mahogany
in this shiny table rots, you can carry on about his heroism
till the Mekong runs dry, you can talk about the books
you both read as students in Paris when you, in your spare time,
screwed the daughters of the upper crust and he, minutes away,
cleaned fish and ate soup made from their boiled heads.
You can look him in the eye till you forget what a smile means,
you can promise him a bridge over every
pathetic dry run that ever caught and carried
a single drop of jungle piss,

but you'll never get him to give up
because there'll always be another soldier,
another young buck with a hole for a heart
or a dream he doesn't know enough to mind dying for,
and there'll always be somebody up front shouting
"Follow me!"
whether messiah or madman or hero he be.

For the Historians of War

Make it thick with maps so
we know where they died.

Make it rich with words so
we know how they tried.

Make it louds with song so
we don't hear how they cried.

Make it plain as dirt so
we know how they lied.

Armistice

for EG

The war was dead a decade
and we were still alive.
Crazy Ed's purple heart spawned
cosmic-egg murals on a barren moon,
splattered day-glo flowers into deep space,
but now he sells wildlife prints
to sportsmen's magazines.
My brother quit writing plays,
cut his hair for steady work.
I took a foxhole job,
the camouflage of
standard-issue green.

The war is dead;
we lay down our arms,
we sue for peace in marriage and mortgage,
we march home alone on rutted roads
to fleeting sleep,
to guerrilla dreams,
to the nightmare of capture.

Memorial Day 2016

As if putting flowers,
however beautiful, on
dead soldiers' tombstones
made right that they are dead
due to the folly of high-placed fools
who never got so much as a sock wet
while soldier boys they sent lived and died in that
slop.

Tell me again about those flowers
and those tombstones and
those dead boys and
why.

Regarding Iraq

Zarqawi,
before he got religion and
made it big as a murderer,
was so everywhere tattooed
that they called him, in prison, the Green Man,
covered in every color but
that of blood. Not wanting to displease
his new-found god and wanting still more
to find favor with similarly bold men, the thug
removed his tattoos by himself, one at a time,
with a razor.

Now, Mr. President, you and your generals,
who fear him now that he's out
and has made it big as a murderer
and has a big following,
you tell me
how anyone
can win any battle
against a soldier like that.

V. The Holy

Crickets

Crickets, he'd just read,
eat parts of one another
while copulating, as do
praying mantises,

and he'd read lately, too,
about the common housefly
and songbirds,
and how very short their lives are,
even those lucky enough
to make it out of the nest.

And then, nearly laughing out loud,
with a close-to-crazy smile on his face
and time on his hands, he nearly sang,
"It's a wondrous,
mysterious
world
the Lord has made,
isn't it?"—

this from an octogenarian
in the library lazing away final days,
he whose office had been right next
to mine, he who told me some time back
that he was living in his last decade,

and who believes,
who believes,
who believes.

Priestess

Medusan
the raven woman's glare—
I met her at a suicide
and found myself
a-mazed.

Never
again
shall I so love.

Defenders of the Faith

Surrounded by defenders of the faith,
I never before felt so unsafe,
with their words and their ways
so certain of my sin
clutching the Book tightly
so ready to do me in.

Life in the Jungle

The world's biggest flower
blooms in Borneo.
Its petals are six feet across
and smell like rotting flesh.
They live three days
and they die.

My nose tells me
and my bones agree
that something here,
something huge and near,
that something here
stinks like fury.

At the Kitchen Table on the Anniversary of a Death

A year later
it still hurt
like a deep cut,
a wound fresh as
the bottomless bounty of her garden
in the sharp sunshine of early
September, spilling as would
an autumn-ripe tomato
cut with a canning knife
clean in two.

Tears for the moment gone,
we find balm in talk
of the glory of her garden,
brilliant symmetry of gladiola,
fatness of squash and final potatoes,
plump, thumping music of ripe melon;
we find succor in the savor
of this good, good earth
and all we have taken therefrom,
and all that we owe it, each one.

Journeyman Student, Standout at Third
for DM

Agony of Aristotle and blue book,
other-worldly cant of Kant
and categorical whatever
and Sartre's loneliness
lay siege to this boy
who would otherwise be
on God's green grass
if not for this test, these texts
that count so little
next to the certainty of
straight white lines,
dust raked rich and red
under cleated feet,
the sound of the spheres
when bat hits ball
like subject kisses verb,
when horsehide makes love to leather,
comes loudly, consorts snugly and stays,
the verity of curveball that does not hang,
the hope that one does when he hits,
the hope that it rockets the unabstract
distance to dead center,
the knowing that sometimes he can
hit one out, round the bases
and be part of a wholeness
that would make even Aristotle
jump up to cheer
and not give a damn
if he spilled a full beer.

Firepit and Chairs, Seminary Patio

They sat in circles here,
fire before them feeding their eyes,
darkness behind filling
their hearts with wonder and
fear at what sent them here,
whether and when it would come
to take them back, how
it found its way,
how they might find theirs.

Some say it was the stars, though
night's clarity dimmed in daylight and
they could no longer be seen.
Some say it was a trap door, though,
it being night, it was too easy to fall
into, too easy to be the
source of it all, too tidy an answer
for this other-worldly caul.

Others thought less and worked more,
piled more wood on the fire,
steadfastly stared, breathed deep on what
science has since said is
aromatic poison, worse even than
cigarettes; meantime,
the fire burned,
the night reigned
and the stars, the stars,
exactly what we need, are,
in brightest light, exactly what
we cannot see.

After Sappho: A Fragment about Baseball and Love

Fragment 41:
To an army wife, in Sardis:

Some say a cavalry corps,
some infantry, some again
will maintain that the swift oars

of our fleet are the finest
sight on dark earth; but I say
that whatever one loves, is.

Some say the moonshot home run,
some the unhittable kid
all heedlessness and heat;

some say the backhand stab and
strike from deep short, just in time,
some the dust of safe slide home;

some, again, say the slider
that slices a sliver of
corner, some say new-ball white

is the finest sight under
sun or dome or lights; but I say
that whatever one loves, is.

Group Picture

Finally,
we are small and funny-looking,
misshapen and soft,
crammed into clothes
whose forms we have wrinkled and ruined,
gluttonously eaten our way out of.
We sport cowlick and nosehair, ear hair,
crazy coifs of baldness and
soon to be so, we grow gross and hairy
on back and belly, we ooze into
elephantine ears, capacious rears

and yet we love and are loved
like there's no tomorrow
because we hope and fear there will be
and we could not bear it alone.
We kiss and commiserate,
we cling without question to even our oddest others,
we comfort like angels,
like lower-case gods.

For Those Who Believe Not in Miracles

for Eduardo Escobar, Utility Man, Father of Three

Of him baseball history will make
no mention, but that one gleaming summer
he hit 33 doubles,
33 doubles,
that magic number
that magical year.

Sandwiches after the Service

Nothing like white bread and ham
to bring us back down to earth
after all those heavy organ notes
and bad singing and contemplation
of the great black beyond
and the great deal
the preacher says it is;

nothing like a steaming cup
of stout Lutheran coffee
to wash down all that dust-to-dust,
ashes-to-ashes that sounded so like
poetry in the version of King James
but seems a world away
in the paneled church basement
where old ladies
whose hands look life lefse
make sure no table has an empty pot,
cut sponge cake so sweet
you can't turn it down,
worry whether there'll be enough

because a big crowd is starting to come in,
talking small talk with old friends
about how awful cold April can be,
how hard it is to believe
that five minutes ago
we put a good man in the ground
and then came back here
to take our place in line.

Two Haiku at Advent

Sunshine paints them bright,
frames them children of light, these
flowering cowards.

Standing front-pew tall,
they smirk in response and call,
upright liars all.

Parable of the Stranger Passing the Theology Suite
for KS

Angels on the head of a pin,
too many to count—
Jesuits with spear-point intellects,
Franciscans ferociously passive
and all those other orders
split by schism and cleaving only
to their own ancient idea, so much so
that through the haze of hermeneutics
it's hard to tell them apart, hard to find
any hint of gospel truth for those
solely, simply suffering,
heartsick, seeking succor, praying
to be saved.

How long, oh Lord, how long
need they, need we wander this wilderness of
where is God? Dogma is dead bones;
of canon or catechism, let the devil have his say,
let the winner have his way--
I want no more than to find Him;
this child of God merely prays
for a star to find and follow,
for a truth to light my way.

Three Ways

I.
Go on as if nothing happened.
Shave. Tie your tie.
Kiss your pretty wife,
whether awake or asleep
or in dream or real life,
goodbye. Remember
that your routine
remains the same;
those you know and love
will still be themselves,
clocks will run the same circle,
numbers yield the same sum,
yet something is different beyond description
and shall never
not be so.

II.
Hide as long as you can.
Come out only in dire need
or absent any chance of escape.
When asked anything,
deny everything;
say that you never saw, never knew,
never thought through why you should
do anything but
follow along, sing the same song
as those all around you,
glass-eyed and safe.

III.
Do what you can.
Read the age spots on your skin
like a watch, knowing no timepiece
is perfect. Sleep deep; resist
only when it offers some sort of
chance, and know that winning may change
nothing of substance, and that it may
kill you, too. Make your peace
with books lost or long overdue,
with those left on the shelf
you never got to.
Look for a sign in the turn
of each leaf; make sense of the world
as you would a lover's fitful sleep.

Another Way

No.
For a better analysis
see the sun on the water,
see the gleam in a child's eye
or the curve of his spine
that will one day cripple him,
see the tear on the face of a stranger
or a lover, see the red and the blue
of any heart near you
or otherwise,
see the day in its glory,
see the species in its folly,
see the vacant gaze of hope
of a parent whose child is gone,
see the million colors in the single feather
of the most ordinary grounded bird,
see the masterly mosaic pattern
on the wing of a pigeon
fouling the street in front of you,
see the droop of a stately fir
buried in snow that may
break its strong branches
like love, one way or another,
breaks every heart.

Aztec Dream

Lashed awake above dens of adobe
I am found a trespasser
in the Temple of the Sun.
Mute as the desert,
my captors tell me nothing;
they glare accusations of god-kings
ransomed by white men,
black eyes beaming remembrance
of Montezuma. The stare of the lizard
is on the land, and it prevails
in its cold-blooded way,
shapes a verdict in which
I have no say.
Shamans gust curses on gold,
and my hair is the color
of straw.

They Believed

I. The Pagan

He believed in all that snake shit
but he wasn't crazy.
He talked to the sibyls every day,
he told me,
and they talked back and told the truth
every time,
but he wasn't crazy.
He denied flying into that girl's room even though
he knew, from the sibyls, that it could be done, but
he didn't do it, and
he wasn't crazy.

II. The Patriot

He believed in all that Brit shit,
but he wasn't crazy.
It spoke to him, those fields of Eton,
the sun never setting, that pluck and grit,
the flag and the sun on all of it
telling a truth he held tight to,
and he did for it as much as he could do,
a truth the wogs or machines guns never knew,
but he wasn't crazy.

III. The Preacher

He believed in all that God shit
but he wasn't crazy,
what with the gilt-edged pages
promising salvation and rolled-away stones
and the other miracles he'd so long known
but never seen, talking to God and knowing
He was listening even though He
sent no sign,
but he wasn't crazy.

The charge is always true
against all of us
but can't be proven to
the standard we demand,
enlightened moderns
who cite the books we write
to keep us away from the abyss,
to keep us above knowing the dirt on our feet
or believing crazy ideas about how we could fly
or that snakes had anything to tell us
or that sybils or machine guns or gilt-edged pages
could give us or tell us
what we need to get by.

VI. The End

After the Appointment, Watching My Wife of Four Decades Nap

She sleeps longer now,
sometimes even through the
slamming of a door; it if were an
intruder, she'd be a
goner. But it wasn't and
she's not and it's
quiet here now,
and she sleeps deep
but not peaceful. I can tell.

There's something
in this silent, homey air
I've never known before,
here or anywhere,
something I can't name or see,
that's near nonetheless,
that frightens me.

This Banquet of Loss

I.
No symptoms, no trouble at all
except, in the urine,
that little bit of blood
the naked eye can't see
and the learned don't know
what to make of.
"More tests,"
the white coat mumbled;
we waited.
Torturous time passed.
Another bullet dodged,
another crisis abated.

II.
Later, on a sunny day, we learned
that the painter's eye may
burst, or the swelling
may go down, and all might go
back to normal or as close
as we come to whatever that is.
Either way,
this is not over.

III.
What course comes next
in this banquet of loss,
this daily bread of breakdown?
Those we love, barely know, despise,
they fade, still glowing, they sink
like suns going to sleep

behind familiar hills
or explode like gunpowder
dumped into fire.
The obituary pictures are stunning,
proof that those dilapidated and crumbling
were once statuesque and becoming,
smiles, cheekbones, eyes, other parts
that made them knockouts, that would have,
had we been there, made us want
to glory in the gleaming flesh
that now lies beyond repair,
gone or on the way there,
all of us always in the undertaker's care.

IV.
Would that we all could go
the way of old Bilbo Baggins
at movie's end,
meeting at water's edge
a kindly old man in belly-length beard
offering soothing words and promises
that the ship is sturdy and strong
and the shore not far off
and who let us carry aboard
what remains of all we once were
or wanted to be,
strong enough for the trip,
wise, resigned, awake and aware
yet mercifully murky about how we got there
and what is beyond that alluring fog
and its mystery and menace.

V.

But no. Not as Bilbo do we go, but with
coughs and convulsions that would break the
bedframes in which we bucked ourselves born.
Nothing is gauzy here; even morphine leaves clear
the minutiae of all that has gone wrong.
Behind us, the shire is green as ever
as we make our way to the cairns of the unstoried dead,
our holes in the ground
whether cold stone or warm bed.

VI.

In the absence of swelling cellos,
let there be, at last, at least,
some small symphony, some note
of deliverance; let there be lucidity,
some sense of things settling out as they ought, as
in the symmetry of grand trees
in the years before they fall
to axe or illness, as on their way down
they are one with the sky as part of the fall
they know must come, the fall that troubles them
not at all.

Upon Seeing an Old Man Haul a Box of Books Up a Steep Stairs

So light each leaf on its own
but so many to lug so far after so long
is another story;
between these covers
all manner of mirth
and monster,
the sweetness of song,
the coarseness of knives
gone dull with hard use,
the elegance of brushstroke,
the ugliness of nightmare
artistically rendered real ...

All this
bearing down
on the breakable spine
that strains to hold him
on his steep climb,
all this:
Schweitzers and DeSalvos,
all such Alberts and others,
oddballs, angels, animals—
all these stories
that he loves enough
to carry this far,
to bear this long,
how they have on this snowy day
made me more tired

than words can say,
made leaden my young legs,
made an old man's
my heart.

House Made of Bone

The jangling telephone brought no surprise
but cut deep anyway:
An old man was dead, Grandpa gone
three years short of nine decades,
four score and change worth of
stories about horses with names,
ponies that kicked little boys
dead at Christmastime, beautiful hogs
that fetched two-fifty a hundred
when things were as bad as they got,
when it didn't matter a damn how you worked
or tried, when the only way to get by
was to bank on the dumb luck that sometimes
lets you land on your feet whether you
deserve it or not, whatever that means. Grandpa is dead,
my father's father now part of the permanent past tense;
his casket shined like the Buick he never did buy,
and when my young back helped haul him
from the church to the frozen plot where he would lie,
my eyes couldn't leave the numbers, couldn't leave
the names carved on the cold stones
waiting before us.

My daughter died before I knew her,
not out of her mother's sweet belly long enough
to learn to suck, not long enough for us to see
her eyes dance side to side in a world
we thought she would be part of, a world
we thought she would make and take and keep warm.
Molly never had a chance, too weak too early,
put upon by what neither we nor she

could fight or see. It took me
days to cry; I still don't know why.

It dawned on me as I drowsed in the music
of my mother kneading bread how ordinary
were the neighborhood brutes
who took clubs and stones to Slavs and Jews
who had done no more and knew no more
than being alive, and who asked no more than they
be granted a stay, that they be allowed to draw breath
and bake bread and pray to something
in the blackness that gave them pause,
that gave them reason to sing, that gave them anchor,
that gave them cause.

Such is the sin and the sign in a world that spins on regardless:
something taken forever that so lately came,
something we barely knew. And such is the salve:
something on which to hang hope
without reason, something to believe,
something to have. And such is the song
or the sigh or the promise or the lie that says,
I live in a house made of bone,
and I'm learning to feel
right at home.

Lighthouse at Hatteras

for John Berryman, the eminent Dr. Bones

". . . the coast had eroded so much that the sea lapped at the base of the tower, once a safe 1,500 feet from the water. The noble lighthouse was abandoned . . ."

". . . hard on the land wears the strong sea and empty grows every bed." —Dream Song #1

The sea, John, the very sea
that made it legend
lays siege to Hatteras.

Standing on sand,
this one-eyed beacon saved sailors and ships
but cannot save itself
from water an ocean wide,
from the rhythmic terror of a sullen moon's tide.
Little to see from this lighthouse view
but Davy Jones' crapshoot—
no message in a bottle,
no dirge for drowned sailors,
nothing to know for sure but
that some make it,
for now, at least, and
others do not.

And that, Bones,
is the answer, source
of mermaid song,
a verdict of who lives and dies

without a word of how or why—
and you and I,
lighthouse men these many years,
or fancying ourselves so,
stare to the horizon and
watch it come our way;
dizzy in the dumb wind,
moonstruck by the bloodless tide,
we see that even this light,
so old, strong and tall,
is doomed, shall one day surely fall.

Around Forty

The years under our belts
hung over that night,
three men half-full
of wine and counting
best as we could recall
the days not all that long ago
when we, hard of belly,
were told to shoulder rifles
without asking why.
We clicked off years
like ballplayers' numbers,
we talked about women
we never dared talk to,
we laughed at stupid stunts
that could've killed us,
card games where
one dumb bluff
could've clubbed us
to death,
the hit and miss
of bullets flying by,
the dumb luck
that led us, let us
come to that night,
to this knowing,
this look back
we never saw coming,
to a longing that took so long
to feel that we feel old
when we remember
what we never knew.

Too Old to Teach
for AM

He is too old to teach, we're told,
too tired to work anywhere
but in his garden, where
he toils workmanlike waiting for
harvest, knowing it can go
either way, bounty or
bust, fat tomatoes or
cinders, testament to
what once was,
what could have been.

Now he ministers to the dead
and the soon to be so, shuffling in
on his own tired knees, ankles,
feet, but always bearing, always
wearing a smile, though faint it sometimes be,
and good wishes, always good wishes,
strong and true as a young man's
tempered by what he knows, by what he has seen
come and go. His is now
the business of burying or making ready
to do so, of making sure that
what little can be done is, and then

heading home himself,
wheeling his brown Toyota west
onto a busy street, banking on his old eyes,
hoping for the best and muttering prayers
into the glare of the sun
going gorgeously down.

Tibetan Monks Visit Terrace Heights

There are piles of work to do,
but you sit talking
to an old man, killing time,
letting it run through your hands
like sand.

Nearby, someone's child
is about to die of a broken heart
or some other dark dead end
in the warren of woe and want
that is the world we inhabit;
but because it is beyond your reach
you shuffle papers, you run in place as if
you could escape from or file away or seal or heal
the break that is the hole in the world's heart.

And then, as you try to hide from or ignore
such phantoms that haunt and taunt you,
that forever elude, that refuse to
stop and fight or fly away,
the visiting monks, just back from lunch,
appear in blood-colored robes of Zen
and look past you and all you feel so bad about;
wielding metal tools,
they work like worms with infinitesimal grains of sand
and colors to make a picture of the world
that always has at its heart
the mantra that when this gorgeous thing is finished
the wind will sneeze and take it away,
and with it tomorrows and yesterdays,
leaving what is left for only you to say.

Without Name

The old men at the library
smell like cigarettes and
loneliness. They are always last
to leave; like dust in distant corners
they must be found and swept out.
For a little while, it is still warm
where they last sat. Where they go,
what they call home,
Lord only knows.

When the obits run,
we turn the page without slowing,
unable to put faces to
names we never knew.

Coming Home After My 40ᵗʰ High-school Reunion

One who once was a boy remembered both
that the old man of the man who shotgunned
himself had been a mean sonofabitch,
a drunk who beat his wife and kids
who turned out mostly okay
anyway,

and he remembered, too, that
many times in his own house
they ate mush and French toast
because that's what was in the house,
bread bathed in batter from a couple of eggs,
because that's what was in the house,
"and we ate it because it was good
and we got full," realizing only later
how little they had,

but remembering, too, how his mom,
a plump hausfrau who cleaned the school
before she cleaned her own little house,
how she hugged them like they were all
there was in the world.

Somewhere between that shotgun blast and those hugs
and the way they last forever,
somewhere in the middle of that mush and French toast
still warm after all those years
and more savored now than when fresh from the griddle,
somewhere in all that is what we came to know
of life so late in life, what no one could've taught us
when we were still in school.

Pastoral

Clichés clamber out
like fat women from shiny cars,
so many poems are not written
for fear they will be written off
as too prosaic,
so rooted in Mother Earth's
mealy black dirt
that they might crumble like a jilted lover
if someone says they're not true.
So this poem may not be for you,
but if you would hear a homely story,
listen:

My father had bronze arms
and a supple heart.
He taught me timbre
in cutting wood
for building and burning.
He walked his land
like an Indian
and knelt to touch it.
My mother woke me with song
and told me how bright was the sun
or how needed the rain.
She baked and mended and
kept us full and warm.
She hoed her garden clean
in the green heart of summer
and it grew like a meadow.

And you may scoff
or write this off
or tell me to make it new
or say that, for the sad many,
it is not true.
But I will still live
in my strong wood house,
still have morningsong
to wake to.

The Way of Old Men

The cars of their youth roll by
as classics in parades or
wrecks tailing tow trucks,
and the old men
leaning on fences they
are too old to mend
take it all in and see in it
something about which
they say nothing or
nothing we can know.

They have bled through
a half-century of shaving cuts,
they miss swaths of whiskers
and, if told, don't care;
they often wear a wisp of dressing
between mouth and stubble, they
chew too loud, they are followed
wherever they go by a
seat-of-the-pants shininess
they do not know; they warmly remember
houses torn down years ago.

Perhaps this is the way of old men,
to stand and talk too long
when there is work still to be done,
to take our fathers' poses
without seeing ourselves
or the men we unwittingly mimic,
to lament what is gone, to long for
and fear what is yet to come,

to be always on the brink of tears
at the music in church
and all those notes we never once,
never will, hit, to see in every
budding and sagging breast both
beauty and sadness,

possibility and inevitability,
promise and fate, longing and wait
and the weight of it all, the sky on
our shoulders, the sun on our balding heads,
the years on our dreams and all
we thought we knew and that we can do
next to nothing about, we who
once saw ourselves as those who
had to do what a man had to do;
if we ever cry, it is when no one
will look or see; we keep track
by writing numbers in little books
no one will ever read, keeping our own tally
of what life gave and gives, our own toll
of what life takes, of what life took.

Good-night Kiss

We bathe in the same water,
drink from the same cup.
We have been naked for so long
in front of each other that
the ridiculous no longer registers--
tufts of hair, folds of skin
showing up where
they've not before been.
We know each other's night sounds,
whether they mean nightmare or dream,

and we know that one day one of us
will not wake from this,

which is the sweetness
and the terror
of every good-night kiss.

Acknowledgements

Grateful acknowledgement is made to the editors of the journals and anthologies in which the following poems originally appeared:

"Child Fear" in *Rag Mag*, Black Hat Press, Goodhue, Minn., Vol. 14, No. 1, Fall 1996.

"Runner" and "For Such Women" in *Loonfeather*, Bemidji, Minn., Vol. 13, No. 1, Spring/Summer 1992.

"In a Stranger's Bathroom" in *The Toilet Papers*, Pueblo, Colo., Arts & Academic Press, 1994.

"Armistice" in *Witness*, Serengeti Press, Mississauga, Ont., Canada, 2004.

"Journeyman Student, Standout at Third" in *Elysian Fields Quarterly*, Knothole Press, St. Paul, Minn., Vol. 20, No. 4, 2003.

"Upon Seeing an Old Man Haul a Box of Books Up a Steep Stairs" in *Java Snob Review*, Bellevue, Mich., Summer 1997.

"Around Forty" in *ArtWord Quarterly*, White Bear Lake, Minn., No. 6, Fall 1996.

The following poems previously appeared in *Gone Away from Crystal Valley*, a self-published collection, 2010:

"Beatitude: Cycle of Water"

"Letter to a Lover"

"Sandwiches after the Service"

"Pastoral"

"Imprint: High Ways and Low"

"At the Kitchen Table on the Anniversary of a Death"

"Something for a Son"

About the Author

Steven Schild lives in Winona, Minnesota, with his wife Margaret. They have two grown sons, Jake and Sam. Schild's poetry has appeared in a number of literary magazines and four anthologies and has won awards from Viterbo University and the League of Minnesota Poets. His collection *Eros in Autumn* was awarded a Silver Medal in the 2014 by the Midwest Independent Publishers Association, and his manuscript *Erotic Tales of the Root River Conference, Now Defunct* received an Honorable Mention in the Acorn-Rukeyser Chapbook competition in 2005.

www.ingramcontent.com/pod-product-compliance
Lightning Source LLC
Chambersburg PA
CBHW022028090426

42739CB00006BA/330